THE VINTAGE
OF
SPIRITUALITY
The Passage is the Destination

THE VINTAGE OF SPIRITUALITY
The Passage is the Destination

Sarbjit Singh Chhina

Lithouse

2021

The Vintage of Spirituality: The Passage is the Destination
— Published by Lithouse, Delhi.

© Author, 2021

ISBN: 978-93-90569-10-6

Laser typeset by
Lithouse, Delhi.

Contents

Contents

1

Passage _
The True Destination

According to spiritual saints, Creator is the origin; Creator is the sustainer and Creator is the destination.

- ◊ Creator has no name but creation is identified by names.

- ◊ Creator is one but creation is infinite.

- ◊ Creator has no form but creation is in infinite forms.

- ◊ Power and pelf are temporary as creation is temporary.

There is a story that when God created human beings, human beings started disturbing God. God was perturbed. God tried to hide in different places. He went to a hill, then to a faraway place in the sky, and then under the ocean, but humanity looked for him everywhere. Ultimately, he concealed himself in the inner soul of the human being.

Human beings have since times immemorial been searching for the Creator and whenever human beings attain success in searching for him in their inner self, they merge with the Creator and are not separated from the Creator.

That is why nobody can reveal anything about the Creator. Whatever is visible, that is perishable. Whosoever is born shall die.

In the words of saints, the Creator is never born and never dies. Creator was there, prior to creation and Creator will be there after creation. Soul is in the inner self, the lock is closed from inside. The lock is to be opened from the inner self by entering in the inner. There is a passage to enter the inner self. This passage is the destination to turn the mind under the soul.

And only the Creator is permanent

Creator is invisible in the invisible soul

Creation is visible in the visible universe.

According to mystics meditation – Remembrance of Creator, is the passage and it is also the destination. It is in the inner self of the soul. Nobody has found God on a hilltop or on some star. If anybody has found God, he has found it in his inner self.

Always remember the Creator,

Creator is permanent,

Creation is perishable.

2

It is Too Late

There was a courtier in the court of an Arab king. His son was brilliant in education and had a spiritual bent of mind. He had the influence of spiritual saints on him. His father was very ambitious, he had good relations with the king and persuaded the king for his son to be appointed as a minister in his cabinet. On the other hand, the son was very simple and he had no ambition of worldly power and pelf and he was always busy in meditation – remembering the Creator. On the persuasion of the father, the king asked his courtier to bring the boy to the royal court. So when father and son appeared before the king, without even taking a proper look at him the king turned towards the courtier and said: "Go and come back after a year."

Father and son returned home. As usual the boy continued with meditation for a very long time of the day. He had become desireless. But after a year they again went to the king. After looking at them for a moment the king asked the father to come after a year. This went on for a long time.

The boy continued with meditation, remembrance of the Creator for the most part of the year. He wanted to divert his mind away from worldly pleasures and concentrate on the Creator, but his father was anxious that his son get appointed as a minister. The family would enjoy power and importance.

After about three years, the king called the courtier suo-moto and asked him to bring his son so that he may join as a minister. The pleasure of the father was limitless. He went home immediately to break the news. But his son refused to accept this invitation from the king. The father was hurt and no persuasion helped in chaging the decision. The father became sure that his son would not join.

He reported everything to the king. The king found it strange, he himself went to see the boy, and once he met him he saw the strange spiritual aura on his face. He was impressed and again requested the boy to join as a minister.

But the boy politely said, "Sir I am thankful to you but you have come too late. I have no desire for any worldly power and pelf and whatever I have realized that is worth hundreds of kingdoms. I am sorry I cannot join."

Physically the boy was the same without any change. He had changed in his inner. His realization was not comprehensible to his father and to the king. But it was his inner transformation and this transformation was not in external appearance but it was in the inner the spiritual path. It is the same for everyone, anybody living at any place, speaking any language, performing any profession but it is one, for everyone, According to saints, true spiritual wealth is in the inner self. Worldly wealth is outside.

By bowing one's head, the questions and worries finish. By arrogance, questions and worries arise. By looking down to the earth, questions and worries end, by looking at the sky questions and worries arise.

Always remember the Creator,

The Creator is permanent,

The creation is perishable.

3

Importance of Organs

There is a story that life is based on the soul. It is said that in ancient times all the organs of the human body could speak and one day they disputed on their importance. Every organ claimed that one is more important than the other. As all the organs were quarrelling, someone suggested that as "Brahma" is your creator, it is better to meet Brahma and let him judge. So they went to Brahma and put their case before him.

"Brahma" listened to their arguments and decided that all the organs would have to go out from the body and then enter the body one by one and their importance would be judged by their performance.

So all the organs were separated from the body and then started entering the body one by one. Ultimately the whole body was ready, but still it was not functioning. No organ could function; the body was lying still. Then "Brahma" asked the soul, to enter the body.

Though the soul is formless but once it entered the body all the organs started functioning. Now all the organs realized their helplessness without the formless soul.

The mystics have prescribed that the soul can live without a body but body cannot live without a soul. Formless soul is a part of super soul. Soul has to join the super soul, body is not to join the super soul. Soul is striving to join the super soul, that is not born and does not die. The mind is a wave, the soul is an ocean. Wave is born and finishes, the ocean is permanent. The soul is a part of the super soul.

Body desires that the soul may not leave it but the soul is within the body by the order of the Creator. It enters and leaves by the order of the Creator. The soul is the centre of the body.

Everybody has a different centre. But every soul has one centre – super soul. In the words of mystics, body cannot join super soul only formless soul can join formless super soul.

Consciousness has to develop into super consciousness, but this consciousness is in the inner self and therefore there is need to cultivate the inner self. As the soul an invisible consciousness is also invisible, consciousness will develop as super consciousness. This development is made in stages. Super soul – the Creator is remembered by the name of the Creator. The name by which we call the Creator is different for different people, but realization of the Creator, the super soul is the same for every soul.

Sufi Saint Nizamuddin was strolling along with his followers on a river bank. Some people were throwing water towards the sky, the follower laughed, Nizamudin asked why he was laughing. The follower replied, that they are searching for God by throwing water into the sky. Nizamuddin said, it is their way. It is not the way or the rituals or the words or the language, it is the spirit of the action, that should be directed towards the search of the Creator. One should have the Creator in mind, it is the path of reaching the Creator that is important.

The body is made up in time and it would finish in time. But the soul was not made in time and it would not finish in time.

According to mystics, spiritual development is not related with the development of the body. It is enlightenedness that is related to the soul and not the body.

Always remember the Creator,

The Creator is permanent,

The Creation is perishable.

4

Power of Wealth

When Alexander was on his death bed he realized that he could not survive even by paying all his wealth and his empire, death was imminent. He invited all his courtiers by his bedside and instructed them to follow his orders and said:

1. While carrying my body to the graveyard, all the famous doctors of the world, who had been treating me should proceed my coffin, so that the people may become aware that no medicine and no doctor can secure a human being from death, howsoever powerful one may be or how much wealth one may possess.

2. While moving towards the graveyard, please continue to throw all my wealth on both sides of my coffin that I amassed in my life, so as to show that wealth amassed by any means is useless and nobody can carry it; wealth does not give any security.

3. While carrying my coffin to the graveyard, please place both my hands out of my coffin so that the people may know that nobody can carry even a penny with him after his death.

According to saints, worldly wealth is perishable, spiritual wealth is permanent. Worldly wealth is related to the comforts of our body, spiritual wealth is related to bliss of the soul. As the body is temporary, so worldly wealth is temporary, but the soul is permanent, so spiritual wealth is permanent. Worldly wealth is limited, spiritual wealth is unlimited. Alexander had amassed a lot of worldly wealth but he was ignorant of spiritual wealth. Many kings belong to the outside world but enlightendness belongs to the inner world and is related to spiritual development.

According to saints there is an original house that belongs to the soul, once a person returns to his house, he is only interested to reach his or her home. And not interested in the pleasures and plays of the passage.

In the words of mystics the Sufis, the saints, the enlightened souls made efforts, to search for the soul, to be enlightened. That enlightenedness belongs to the inner, not to outer but available with the grace of the creator.

Always remember the Creator,

The Creator is permanent,

The creation is perishable.

5

Price of Bliss

There lived a great and kind king named Premjit. He had a vast empire, army and wealth. He added new territories to his kingdom. But as he grew old he realized that his end was near. He became frustrated and his frustration escalated day by day. He shared his frustration with his close friends and advisors.

He was advised to see a faqir who lived near his capital. The faqir had a spiritual aura around him which reflected on his face. He was respected; and it was even said that he was immortal. One could realize bliss even by glancing at him, he had no fear of death.

One day he went to the faqir with his advisors and he enjoyed a different and a strange sensation of bliss, just by looking at him. There was a divine smile on his face. The king placed a number of costly gifts at his feet. But he did not care and directed him to meet his disciple.

The king saw the disciple and told him his problem. He even asked the disciple that if this bliss that he could feel could be transferred to him at any price he would be willing to pay it. He began visiting the faqir regularly and made the same request. The disciple raised the price of the bliss and ultimately the king became ready to give up even his entire kingdom. Then the disciple told the king that perhaps the king had not recognized him. He was also a king and was holding an empire, much bigger than his.

But what the disciple had gained, could be earned by spiritual development. It cannot be purchased even by the whole wealth of the world. In the opinion of saints, enlightenedness is in the inner, inner cannot be transferred,

Remembrance of one Creator is devotion.

The Creator is remembered by his name.

It is to be earned by one's devotion on the spiritual path but by the grace of the Creator only.

Outward wealth can be transferred, inner wealth cannot be transferred.

Always remember the Creator,

The Creator is permanent,

The creation is perishable.

6

Tree of Virtue

Once a sage was giving his discourse, he said that there is a tree of virtue, and who ever gets an opportunity to eat the fruit of that tree, would attain immortality. But it was very hard to locate that tree. A king was listening to that discourse. The thought of immortality and the tree of virtue haunted him. He sent his people to find that tree of virtue, but there was no sign of such a tree anywhere. Now that saint had gone and no trace of that saint was with them.But the idea of the tree of virtue of immortality haunted him perpetually.

After about seven years, one day the king was on a hunting expedition. He caught sight of the same saint and rushed to him and enquired about that tree of virtue as told by him and he explained that his men had looked for that tree everywhere in jungles, hills and in all his kingdom but failed in their endeavour. But the saint said that it was not outside anywhere on earth or, on any star or on any mountain or anywhere in the world.

The king pleaded with him to know where he could find the tree. The saint said, it was in his inner. It is in everybody's inner, but it is required to be explored. But as the king was desperate for immortality, he wanted to know how it could be explored. The saint said, it is only human beings, who are afraid of death. Animal and birds have no fear of death. Even when an animal is going to be slaughtered he enjoys the grass on the way. Actually, only human beings are conscious of death.

But death is imminent, it is not that one may deplete his or her consciousness like an animal rather one should turn their consciousness into superconsciousness. On the other side, the human being with super consciousness is not afraid of death. Saint considered it as homecoming and as bliss and this is the virtue that is available only by the grace of the Creator.

According to the mystics, body was made in time it would be extinguished in time too, either you are saint or a common person but the soul was not made in time, so it would not finish in time. The saint explained to the king that soul merges with the super soul that is the fruit of virtue and it is in our inner. The inner is to be developed, but it is available only with the grace of the Creator. But one must strive to obtain it without caring for the results.

Saint said to the king, the man sitting on the train is aware that the train will stop at the station he has to get off but expects a comfortable journey. Similarly, a human being should live comfortably. The wealth, pelf and power and the kingdom is not long lasting, but our soul is not perishable. The remembrance of the Creator is the fruit of virtue that fruit is within our inner and not outside and it is available by our spiritual labour. It is the passage and it is the destination. The seeker has no desire and it is available with the grace of the Creator.

In the words of mystics, the physical and material comforts are related to the body, but those are temporary. But spiritual comforts as related to the soul are permanent.

Remember the Creator,

Creator is permanent,

Creation is perishable.

7

Three Saints with a Short Prayer

There were three saints living on the bank of a river. They said very short prayers and hardly spoke. In these prayers, they were giving thanks to the Creator. Their prayer was from the core of their inner being. There was a special spiritual aura on their faces. The people were impressed by their aura and their utterances. More and more people came to them. People thought that they have, some supernatural powers within them, but they always denied such powers and only prescribed honest living and to care for every human being irrespective of race, religion, but to remember the one permanent

Creator. Remembrance of the Creator by his name. This name may be different for everyone – but its realization is the same for everyone. It was the same in the past, same at present and will remain the same in future.

But on the other side, there was a senior priest of the city who was well educated and knew a lot of religious philosophy and history. He was a very learned person.

He was aware of the popularity of those saints and he was jealous why so many people visited them.

One day the senior priest was furious and after crossing the river went to the three saints. The saints paid full respect to the senior priest, but the senior priest reprimanded them that they did not know anything about religious philosophy, history and did not know the long prayer. They should prohibit people from coming to them.

The three saints expressed that it is not the length of the prayer that is important, not the words but the spirit of faith without uttering a word but the three saints accepted their ignorance and said that they did not know anything. They had little knowledge about the world. They only knew the name of the Creator and remember only the Creator who is permanent. And this was their message to the people who visited them. They did not know any long prayer, the senior priest uttered and rather they would start coming to him to learn the long prayer.

The three saints, agreed to every condition put forth by the senior priest and agreed to come to him from the next day onwards, so that spiritual secrets may be learnt by them. The three saints came to see him off at the river bank. He boarded the boat but in the middle of the river the boat capsized and the senior priest was in danger of drowning.

The three saints saw his plight and they ran towards him. The senior priest saw the three saints running on river water, without drowning and were wonder- struck. The three saints helped him and brought him on the other side of the bank of the river.

But on the other side of the bank, the archpriest fell on the feet of the three saints and requested them to teach him the short prayer, they were saying.

More than 20 million books are written on religion but faith on Almighty is a common factor in all these books. According to mystics, nobody can unravel the mystery of creation and Creator, if anybody goes to the core of truth he/she merges in the Creator.

Spirituality is related to the inner self, whatever is in the inner cannot be located outside.

According to mystics if one knows much outside he/she acquires knowledge about creation. If one knows more about inner self he/she becomes knowledgable about the Creator.

Kindness is the basis of every religion. All religions agree in the concept of – one Creator but countless people have been killed in the name of religion, but religion believes in one God, who residers in every religious place. If people are killed meaninglessly then how can the path to God be secured which resides in the inner self of every one.

> *Always remember the Creator,*
>
> *The Creator is permanent,*
>
> *Creation is perishable.*

8
Value of Master's Shoes

Nizamuddin was a great saint and respected by everyone. One day one of his disciples went to him and requested for financial help as he was in dire need of money for the marriage of his daughter. Nizamuddin offered to give him all the donations he would be receiving for three days. But it so happened that no donations came to him for those three days.

The man was upset, but Nizamuddin gave him his shoes and told him to sell them and fulfill his needs. He proceeded towards his house but he was frustrated that who would purchase these shoes. He was depressed and crushed by financial burden. He slowly trudged towards his house with a heavy heart.

Amir Khusro who was also a disciple of Nizamuddin was returning from Kabul along with camels which were loaded with goodies that he had brought from that place.

He smelt the presence of his guru's belongings and he shouted to locate them. Ultimately he saw a man carrying the shoes of his guru. Amir Khusro went to him and offered to give all the loaded material in exchange for those shoes of his guru. It was altogether strange for that man.

Amir Khusro had realized that worldly things are temporary but guru's blessings are permanent. But the simple man was not aware about the guru's blessings.

According to mystics, enlightened persons have earned their inner peace on the spiritual path with meditation. Remembrance of the Creator is important but enlightenedness is available by the grace of God. It can be earned by the rich and poor in east and west and by the king or a commoner or anybody without any reference of status.

The spiritually awakened or enlighted person belongs to all religions, or to no religion. He belongs to all the nations or to no nation. According to mystics this spiritual light cannot be seen by physical eyes, that can be realized by soul and not by mind.

According to saints enlightenedness was earned by Buddha and others in all the ages. It could be earned in one's own house or anywhere, but it has no condition of any location. It can be earned in a forest or in a city or anywhere. Ravi Dass Ji, Guru Nanak Dev Ji and other saints remained confined to their jobs.

Enlightenedness is not related to the body. It is related to the soul. Pleasures of mind are temporary pleasures of soul are permanent.

The mystics describe the body as temporary, its pleasures are also temporary. As soul is permanent its pleasures are also permanent.

Always remember the Creator,

The Creator is permanent,

Creation is perishable.

9

Power of Faith

There was a saint who was known for his spiritual aura and many people visited him. But he did not claim any spiritual power as he spent most of his time in meditation. He had a number of disciples who were also practising meditation, remembering the Creator through their soul.

It so happened that one of his disciples could walk on water, without drowning. Even if he fell from the mountain he would not be hurt.

Most of the disciples of the saint were of the impression that the saint had given him such powers. So the other followers insisted that they should also be given that power that they may also walk on water. But the saint had been denying that neither he had any power nor had he given this power to anyone. But he was only prescribing that remembrance of the Creator who is ever permanent, is the only message he had been giving.

But as the disciples did not believe and insisted that he walk on water.

On being persuaded by his disciples, the saint stepped on water and almost drowned when disciples came to his rescue and he was saved.

The disciples were amazed at what had happened, when his disciple can walk with faith on his master, his master, cannot walk with him. But the master declared that the faith of my disciple is perfect on his master and my faith is not perfect for my master. Because of the perfect faith of his disciple, he is able to walk on water, but because of the master's tottering faith he could not walk.

Faith is power but shaking faith is not power, only super soul is the object of traveller to reach the inner path.

In the words of mystics spiritual wealth can be earned by spiritual pursuits – remembering the

Creator but only with the grace of the Creator. But worldly wealth can be earned by worldly pursuits.

Spiritual wealth belongs to the soul. Worldly wealth can be enhanced by gathering more and more money. But spiritual wealth can be enhanced by distributing more and more of spiritual wealth.

Always remember the Creator,

The Creator is permanent,

The creation is perishable.

10

Value of Breath

Alexander was a great king, he won a number of countries and territories. He dreamt of conquering the whole world. In this pursuit he attacked, one or the other country in which lakhs of people were killed either on his own side or the enemy countries. One day he saw a fakir, lying on the ground, but the glow and aura on his face was so attractive that Alexander could not go a step further and went near the saint and enquired the secret of the flowing bliss on his face to which the fakir replied, he was out to win the world to earn bliss but one cannot earn bliss even by winning the whole world. But if you would have won over your heart you would have enjoyed the bliss equal to the victory of the whole world. But to win a heart, you have to go into your inner and not anywhere else. It is not necessary to march to different countries with forces, horses, elephants and weapons etc. By winning the whole world you cannot enjoy bliss. But by winning your mind that is in your inner you can have bliss more than the victory of the world.

Alexander, however, continued with warfare. At the young age of 32, he fell ill and he had to leave his pursuit and return home. On the way he fell victim to a disease and recovery seemed impossible.

Once he lost hope of ever recovering, he called all the doctors and requested that he would give half of his empire to any doctor who would enable him to meet his mother. But all the doctors told him in one voice.

"Even if you give whole of your empire, nobody can grant you even a single breath."

He remembered the words of the fakir. He realized the importance of life and breath that is not visible. He was unable to get a single invisible breath even with the whole of his visible wealth, power and pelf.

That rule, the power and pelf was temporary. He spent all his time on earning transient power but failed to devote his time and energies to acquire spiritual wealth which would last forever. According to saints, one should strive to get, what is permanent and not what is temporary. True spiritual wealth can be acquired by focusing on our inner. Outer comforts are only temporary in nature.

The inner comforts are permanent, these are related to the soul. Many kingdoms had been thrown away when inner is being explored by kings, but no saint had left the spiritual path to gain a kingdom. It is said that when Alexander was buried his mother used to visit his grave every day crying for her beloved son Alexander – Alexander – Alexander, but one day a voice came from the graveyard.

Mother which Alexander are you calling. "Alexander the great king – my son, whom I am calling," replied the mother. Then again the voice came, "Mother countless Alexanders and kings are buried in these graveyards." Kings are not remembered, but the lamps are burning on the graves of the faqirs.

According to saints, among the living creatures, only human beings have spiritual consciousness – birds, insects and animals have no spiritual consciousness. Human beings are capable of realizing the Creator, other creatures do not have the opportunity. Human beings can earn spiritual wealth. If Alexander would have won, the entire world, still he would have been disturbed because his mind was disturbed and had no control over his soul. But if he could have won the mind and would have put his mind under the control of soul, he would have enjoyed the bliss of winning the whole world.

In the words of mystics if you know about the world, you would be powerful in the world. If you know about yourself you would be powerful over self. As you enter deeper and deeper in your inner, one becomes more and more enlightened.

Always remember the Creator,

The Creator is permanent,

Creation is perishable.

11

Thanksgiving by an Artist

Tansen was the royal musician in the court of Akbar. It was said that Tansen could cause rain by his music and could light lamps with the power of his melodious music.

One day Akbar said to him, "I suppose there is no match for your music. But you must have learnt this art from your master, I want to see your master and listen to his music."

Tansen explained to the king that it was difficult. He said, "My master lives on the river bank alone. He mostly sings at night, when nobody is listening to him, if we wish to listen to his song, we have to go to the river bank at midnight and must hide ourselves at that time. Because if my master becomes aware that somebody is listening to him he will not sing."

But the king was so desperate to listen to the music of his master, that he was prepared to go to the river bank and hide to listen to the music of his master.

Around mid-night, the master came to the bank of the river. He was quite visible in the moonlit night, wearing very simple clothes. He was carrying his musical instrument with him. He sat on the grass under the sky full of stars.

Once he started his sweet song, the emperor was so engrossed that he forgot his kingdom and whole of the world.

Late at night, he returned to his palace, but while returning, the king was so overpowered by his emotions that he could not speak a single word and went to sleep.

Next morning he called Tansen and asked him that while comparing his music with his master, it was like difference between sky and earth.

Your master is at the level of the sky and you are on the earth. His songs provide a strong type of bliss and asked him why it was so?

Tansen explained, that his master sang to thank the Creator for the blessings, but he sings to earn a comfortable living. "My master never sings for admiration, but I sing for popularity and to earn praise."

That the music of his master erupts from his soul, while his music erupts from the mind. Devotional music is concerned with one Creator. Even animals, birds enjoy music and so do snakes the poisonous living being. This phenomenon cannot be explained with logic.

Music has no language, or all languages are of music. Nature enjoys music including flora and fauna, why the head moves in singing cannot be explained as it is related to the soul. It is said that music is the language of the soul.

According to saints being in a state of bliss is no desire, no demand for power and pelf. As bliss is related to soul. Spirituality is related to the soul.

Logic is related to mind, where logic finishes, spirituality starts. The worldly material can purchase comforts and luxuries but worldly things cannot purchase spiritual bliss.

The mystics have described that worldly honours provide happiness but worldly honours cannot provide – bliss, unenlightened person is more concerned about material wealth but an enlighted person is concerned about spiritual wealth only.

Always remember the Creator,

The Creator is permanent,

Creation is perishable.

12

Love of Creator
for Creation

There was a rich farmer. He had two sons. The father had equal love for both, but it seemed that he had more love for his younger son. The elder son remained busy in farming most of the time, but the younger son was always playing with his friends. As he grew in age, his friends began instigating him to get his share from his father's property and start some lucrative business in the city. His father always dissuaded him from such thoughts and did not want his son to go away.

Ultimately under pressure of the younger son, the father divided the property and the younger son sold out everything and went to the city in search of some business. His friends enjoyed theatre, cinema and other pleasures with his money. Soon he was left with almost nothing and his friends started leaving him one by one. He exhausted all his money and now he had nothing to eat, his clothes too were worn out. He had no alternative other than to seek a manual job. But no job was available, ultimately he secured a job in a pig farm, on the condition that he would be staying in the pig farm and would eat whatever is left in the house. He was given the task to take care of the pigs for the entire day.

One day while the pigs were grazing, he thought of his condition, clothes worn out and he cut a sorry figure. His hat much loved by his father too was torn and he had no means of either replacing the hat or his clothes. Then he thought of his father who had a number of servants and knew that his servants were living a better life than him, and decided to return to his father and request him to employ him as one of his servants.

While the younger son had departed, the father would sit on the stairs of his big house and look towards the door, and wait for the return of his dear son.

One day he saw a figure approaching his house far away, he seemed just like his son. He ran towards him and met his son warmly. He saw that the clothes of his son were torn, his hat was in a bad shape. Father kissed his son, ordered for new clothes, a new hat and a gold ring for him. He wanted to celebrate his homecoming by inviting all the villagers to his house.

When the older son saw celebrations in his house and came to know the reason for the celebrations, he was annoyed. Even though he was called by a number of people, he did not come into the house.

Then the father himself went to the fields consoled his older son and told him that as he had lost his younger son, but now he had found him, so he should also join in the pleasures of his brother's homecoming and that celebrations would not be complete till he joined. Even though the son had left him the father's feelings of love for him were the same. The love of the father erupted from his soul and not from the mind.

In the words of mystics all creation is related to its origin, the centre. Creator has equal relations with all creation. If Creator is one how can the creation be different?

The feelings of love are invisible and cannot be explained. These feelings are being realized. Father had equal love for both the sons but this could not be explained in words. The bliss to see his lost son came from his inner being, from his soul.

Human beings enjoying bliss will spread bliss. Bliss cannot be expressed. Bliss is the same for everyone. It is same in all the places and at all times. That can only be realized and cannot be expressed.

Worldly knowledge can be expressed in all the languages and in all words, but spiritual knowledge cannot be expressed in any language or in any words.

According to mystics, the seeker of truth is not interested in results. He is interested in remembrance only. Just as every father has the same relation for his sons, the Creator has the same relations for his Creation.

In the words of saints the bliss available by remembering the Creator is the same either one is rich or poor, either a ruler or ruled, but it cannot be expressed, it is realized only.

Always remember the Creator,

The Creator is permanent,

Creation is perishable.

13

Inheritance of Buddha
(Enlightened)

After a long time, Buddha returned to Kapila Vastu, the capital of his empire. He had turned a bhikshu. Once his father, saw his son Buddha begging. He was hurt and shocked. He asked his son, "Begging does not behove kings."

But Buddha replied "Father now I am not a king. I am a bhikshu, what spiritual bliss I am enjoying as bhikshu, I did not enjoy as a prince. This spiritual bliss is in my inner, it cannot be purchased by kingdoms of the world."

Buddha's son Rahul came to his father. Buddha hugged Rahul. Rahul asked his father to give his inheritance. But Buddha told him that in worldly affairs one inherits everything of his father at the time of his birth. But in his mission of spiritual path one has to earn inheritance. It cannot be transferred. It is associated with transformation. It cannot be inherited.

The mystics have explained that every enlighted soul wishes to transfer their transformative inner to whole of humanity but he/she cannot transfer it even to one. The enlightenedness of a Buddha, a Sufi and others is the same. Buddha – enlightenedness is a state that is related to the soul, that can be attained by anyone. It is available by devotion but by grace of the Almighty.

The Buddha could not solve the questions which had haunted him that why man becomes ill, why does a man grow old and why does a man die? Even he could not check his own old age and death.

He was enlightened. Death was there, but there was no fear of death. According to mystics only the Creator is permanent, who knows the Creator would never say that he knows. Who does not know, he would say he knows.

Truth is always one, falsehood is infinite. Creator is truth, it is one and it is permanent, creation is perishable and it is infinite.

According to mystics Creator is unknowable, it is not known by physical organs. It is known by soul, but with the grace of the Creator.

Creator was one, and the same in the past, same at present and will remain the same in future. Formless Creator is not born, does not grow in age and does not perish with time, creator is living everywhere and it is living in everyone.

Whatever is permanent – Creator, that is considered as imagination by ignorant and whatever is perishable – creation, that is considered as reality.

Always remember the Creator,

The Creator is permanent,

Creation is perishable.

14

Service of Society _ Remembrance of Almighty

There is a story that an angel was deputed by God to register the names of the people who loved God. That angel visited different locations in the world. There was a man who was doing selfless service for the society in a village but he was unaware about religious rituals and practices. One day he saw a strange light at night. He woke up and saw an angel. He asked him that how he could serve him. The angel asked if he knew anyone there who loves God. But the simple man replied, I know that every one loves God and you should register all the names of the people. Then the angel enquired, "Don't you love God." Then the man replied, "I do not know about God, but I love his creation." And the angel disappeared.

After some days, the same angel appeared again and showed him the list of the people whom God loved and the name of that man was at the top of the list.

In the words of mystics, service to society is service to God. The Creator is one, but Creator is living in his creation. As creation is everywhere so the Creator is also everywhere. Service of society is also remembrance – meditation.

Creator is that truth that lives forever, but worldly things live for a short while. Creation is the image of the Creator whosoever loves his creation loves the Creator, whosoever serves society serves the Creator.

A person serving society believes in the welfare of all, once remembrance is started, other virtues – truth, love, affection, humility, honesty, sincerity, faithfulness, ethical values all follow by remembrance of the Creator.

It is said that Yudhishthira the eldest Pandava in the Mahabharata was sent to bring a bad man and Duryodhan the Kaurava prince was asked to bring a good man. But by evening, Yudhishthira could not find any bad man, because he loved everyone and everyone was good for him but on the other side, Duryodhan could not find a good man because everyone seemed bad to him.

According to Saints the soul of every human being has its centre in the super soul. So all the human beings and creation belongs to the super soul. A spiritually enlightened person never hurts the feelings of anybody. As the Creator resides in the heart of all individuals so once the heart is hurt it is the Creator who is hurt.

Once kindness is shown to creation, it is the kindness shown to the Creator.

Always remember the Creator,

The Creator is permanent,

Creation is perishable.

15

Ignorance

There was a poor woodcutter. He was chopping wood on the outskirts of the jungle and sold them to earn his livelihood. The woodcutter went to a faqir and sought his blessings. But the faqir continued in his meditation and after sometime he opened his eyes and said only a few words, "Go ahead in your inner, you would become rich."

The woodcutter did not understand him. Next day he went inside the jungle and found very costly wood. He started cutting and selling that wood and became rich, in a very short time. His faith on the faqir enhanced further. He again went to the faqir to give thanks and asked for further blessings. The faqir was in a trance. He kept sitting for a long time. When he opened his eyes, the man thanked the faqir and sought his blessings. The answer of the faqir was the same. "Go ahead in your inner." The woodcutter went further ahead in the jungle and found more costly wood. He started cutting and selling that wood. He became richer, and built a big house.

As he was earning more and more money, his worries and his frustration were escalating. He was enjoying a different type of bliss, when he was poor. But now he was restless, nobody respected him, even he had amassed a lot of wealth.

One day again the woodcutter went to the faqir and told him about his abundant wealth but he said that despite wealth he was restless. Then the faqir told him that he had not entered his inner. The bliss, the spiritual wealth lies in your inner in remembrance of the Creator and not outside or inside a jungle. According to saints for spiritual wealth you have to enter in your inner to explore prosperity.

According to saints a spiritually enlightened person never feels restless. He never seeks respect rather he respects everyone – whosoever seeks respect does not receive respect. The respect originates from the inner. The inner traveller does not seek results. Remembrance of Almighty is the only passage and the goal.

In the words of mystics, one has to enter in his/her inner, but your inner is locked from inside and not from outside. You can open the lock only by entering in your inner. It is not based on logic as spirituality begins, where logic ceases. Entering in the inner is called a new birth or the development of new consciousness. Entering in the inner - Remembrance of the Creator walking on the spiritual path provides contentedness in your inner and kindness for the outside.

Always remember the Creator,

The Creator is permanent,

Creation is perishable.

16
Kindness _
Basis for Peace

Einstein who invented the atom bomb was not in favour of its use, as the bomb would cause a lot of destruction, but he was helpless. Trueman President of America decided to use the bomb to defeat Japan.

The bomb caused tremendous destruction. Though America was victorious in the second World War but it was at a heavy cost of human lives.

When someone asked Einstein that how the third war would be fought. There were tears in his eyes and he said I don't know about the third war, but there would be no fourth war as nobody would be there to fight that war. Though Einstein knew about the number of stars in the universe, but he did not know himself. He never tried to enter in his own inner.

Destruction always causes frustration, kindness always brings bliss. A human being who enters in his inner becomes kindness personified. Kindness gives bliss, destruction gives restlessness. Waging of war is the interest of the person, who never enters in his inner.

A person entering in the inner would find the same Creator in everyone's soul. Entering in the inner is the remembrance of the Creator. The human being entering the inner enjoys bliss. The human being looking for outside pleasures invites restlessness.

In the words of mystics the person on the inner travel realizes new realization with every meditation – remembering the Creator – reaching the centre.

It is never heard that somebody had found the Creator on the top of the hill or in some jungle or on any star. But it always heard that whoever had found the Creator he had found the Creator in his/her inner.

According to mystics no wealth or power can change your inner, rather entering in the inner diverts the mind from power and pelf. Nobody else can enter in your inner, only you yourself can enter in your inner.

Always remember the Creator,

The Creator is permanent,

Creation is perishable.

17

Accomplishment
of New Kingdom

Buddha was the son of a great king. He had a large empire, and all the comforts of the world. He was ruling over a vast land. But he was always engrossed in three questions, those were, why a man becomes sick, why a man grows old and why a man dies?

These questions were haunting him day and night. His father was intimated by astrologers that either he would emerge as a great king, who would become popular in the world or he would become a saint and would leave his house and renounce the kingdom. The father was worried over this. He did everything so that his son may take more interest in his kingdom.

One day, he left the palace secretly. Prior to his leaving the palace he hugged his son who was sleeping at that time, but the love of his family could not deter him from leaving.

He went to the jungle, he met a number of saints and practised different ways of meditation. He turned into a skeleton while making these practices. Ultimately he became enlightened.

After he became Buddha – the enlightened and he found the answer to those questions, but could not check sickness, ageing or death.

His consciousness turned into supercon sciousness, sickness, old age or death was not dreadful to him. It was a normal course of nature.

For turning his consciousness into super consciousness he should not have left his house but he devoted all the time on this exploration of his self.

After devoting so much time, he was enlightened. He did not get anything from the external world. He got everything in his own inner. Though while entering his inner he lost his kingdom, worldly comforts and luxuries, but he gained a new kingdom that was in his inner. He had not gained any material wealth, but only spiritual wealth. What he had gained, that could not be purchased by his whole kingdom.

According to saints realization of the Creator, is easy that there is no other thing so easy, because it is in your inner. But it is equally hard that there is no other thing so hard to achieve, because it is related with the transformation of your own mind and nothing is more volatile than the mind. Transformation may happen in your mind in a fraction of a moment or it may not happen in ages.

But once Buddha became enlightened, even he could not check his own sickness, ageing or death. He could not avoid death but he had no fear of death. What enlightenedness Buddha had earned, that can be earned by every passenger on the inner travel. It had been the same in the past and present and it would be the same in future. It is the remembrance of the Creator.

Entering in the inner is labour, but it is not physical labour, it is the labour to turn towards the inner, But the fruit is available with the grace of God.

Always remember the Creator,

The Creator is permanent,

Creation is perishable.

18

Lost Wealth

A king went into a jungle; he went far ahead of his army, accompanying him. Unfortunately, he fell off from his horse and was seriously injured. A woodcutter saw him there and rescued him. He managed to bring him to his hut. He was not aware that the person he rescued was a king. He provided him relief. The woodcutter served the king throughout the night sitting by his bedside. In the morning, the army came there looking for their king.

The woodcutter was engaged in the profession of chopping wood from the jungle and after turning the wood into coal, was selling it in the city. He was living in abject poverty. Once the king felt better, he thanked the woodcutter and gave him a large garden of sandalwood as gratitude for his service.

The woodcutter continued with the practice of cutting wood and after turning it to coal was selling it, in the city. After about two years the king again passed the same way and came to the hut of the woodcutter. He thought that by now the woodcutter must have become rich. But again he saw the woodcutter in the same condition living in poverty. He enquired what he had done with the garden of sandalwood. The woodcutter replied that he was doing the same to turn the wood into coal and selling it in the city. But the king saw that handle of the axe was of sandalwood, he gave that handle of the axe to the woodcutter and told him to sell this handle in the market.

Once the woodcutter went to the city and offered to sell that handle he received unexpected money for that small handle. Then he realized how much wealth he had lost. He became aware of the price of that piece of sandalwood. He realized he had wasted the opportunity and time. He could not explore that opportunity because of his ignorance.

He never tried to learn about the wealth he was given. Nor did anybody intimidate him about the wealth he possessed. Neither did he explore nor he was told by anyone. He was not aware of the value of wealth he had.

According to the saints, the ignorant is unaware about the spiritual wealth that belongs to the soul. As the soul is immortal, spiritual wealth is also not perishable. Enlightenedness is related to spiritual development and not with physical development. Love for creation is related to the soul. This is not a physical phenomenon. It is a spiritual phenomenon. That is related to remembrance of the Creator and service of the creation.

Remember the Creator,

Creator is permanent,

Creation is perishable.

19

Declining Alluring Post

There was a king who ruled over a large empire. He felt that he was ignoring the religious aspects of his public. He thought of appointing a saint as a minister to look after the religious affairs.

The day he declared in his cabinet that he wanted to appoint a saint as a minister in his cabinet and deputed two ministers to visit a particular place on the river bank and select a saint so as to appoint him as a minister. The ministers were asked to have a discussion with the saints and select a spiritual saint who might be brilliant and worthy of becoming a minister.

A thief was listening to the decision of the king and he thought of taking advantage of the situation. Next day he also donned clothes similar to the saint and went to that riverbank.

Two ministers came to that place the next day. They saw different saints, some in state of trance while others were busy in daily chores of life but constantly remembering the Creator. The ministers met the different saints with their proposal and told them their intention, one by one but it was a strange situation that nobody was ready to become a minister and to leave sainthood. Rather they did not take any interest in such a proposal. The thief was also intimated about the decisions of the saints. While returning they met the thief posing as a saint and made him the offer. Meanwhile, the thief had been thinking that no saint was ready to be a minister, so there might be something more alluring than this post. That is why everybody had declined it. It was a new experience for the thief turned saint. But he became ready to think over that proposal and asked for one night's time to give his final decision. The ministers returned to the palace and narrated everything to the king.

It amazed the king that no saint was allured for power and pelf. They were happier in their life as a saint and living in huts on the river bank. The king decided to go to the saint who had promised to think over the proposal. That night the thief saw all the saints busy remembering God.

But in that one night, the thief experienced a transformation and he realized his inner self. The idea occurred in his mind that it is obvious that the saints must be enjoying more bliss in this state than they would be enjoying as the king's ministers.

The next day, the king along with the two ministers went to the thief turned saint and made him their offer. But the saint who pretended to be one, declined the offer and became a saint in reality.

The inner self of that thief had changed overnight. His physical needs remained the same. He could enjoy a more comfortable life by being a minister but what caused this sudden change that occurred in his innerbeing in one day and his conception about physical comforts, power and pelf had changed altogether.

The other saints had reached this stage after devoting years in meditation and trance, but the thief had changed overnight. It was because of the grace of God.

Imagination has no limits but reality has limits. It is a reality that power and pelf is temporary. This realization must have occurred in his innerself.

In the words of mystics, everyone is concerned with his/her innerself. The innerself of one is not known to the other. But realization of the creator in the inner is the same for everyone. The remembrance of the invisible Creator is the same in everybody. But nobody can express this realization in words.

According to the saints, God is formless. Where we can find formless God and which door should we knock to get the prized treasure is a question that has vexed everyone. It is not at any place in the whole universe it is only in the innerself of everyone and realized by remembrance of the name of the Creator.

Though the name of the Creator might be different for everyone, but the realization is the same for everyone. It was the same in the past, present and will remain the same in future.

Always remember the Creator,

The Creator is permanent,

Creation is perishable.

20

Blow of a Flower

Mansoor a spiritual saint declared that he is God. But the administration of the time was against this declaration. He was ordered to be stoned to death. But he was ready to face anything. He had no fear of his death. He was not ready to change his conviction and declaration. Everybody was ordered to hit him by a stone. So everybody was throwing stones at him but Mansoor remained calm even at this time.

One of his close friends Shibli also came there. Though he was aware that he is an enlightened soul but he was afraid of the administration also. He did not want to throw a stone, he threw a flower instead.

When Mansoor saw that his friend had thrown a flower Mansoor cried out loudly. The crowd was aghast, why did he cry on being hit by a flower when stones hurled at him did not have any effect.

He was asked why he cried when he was hit by a flower though he remained calm even when stones were being hurled at him. He replied that his friend was aware about him and his flower hurt him. The other people were ignorant, they were not aware, so he could not be hurt by their stones.

When Jesus Christ was crucified he felt no pain. When he was asked to say what he felt for the people who were crucifying him, he said, he prayed to God, to forgive them as they were not aware of what they were doing. These are the feelings of an enlightened soul. These feelings are in the inner of the enlightened soul. This is the innerself, remembrance of the Creator that is same for every soul.

According to mystics, realization of the innerself is the same for everyone, it was same, millions of years ago and it will remain the same millions of years later on. Creation is a continuous process but the Creator is the same. The outerself of everyone is different even thumb impression of everyone is different. But innerself of everyone is the same.

Rituals direct the mind to enter our innerbeing. If the innerself is not clear, it leads to wrong living. Rituals are related to the discipline of the mind. Rituals help to put the mind on the path of inner travel - remembrance of God, so that the mind may come under the control of the soul.

In the words of mystics, innerself cannot be transferred. Nobody can enter in the innerself of the other, but one can in his own innerbeing by remembering the Creator.

Always remember the Creator,

Creator is permanent,

Creation is perishable.

21
Feeling of Fulfillment

There is a story that a king was afraid of death. His fear of death escalated as he grew older. Somebody told him that there is water flowing from a fountain on top of the hill and anybody who drank that water would become immortal. But it is difficult to search for that fountain and it is very difficult to reach the top without risking one's life.

With great difficulty the king was successful and found the fountain. He was just going to drink the water, when he heard a voice.

"Do not drink water." The king turned to hear from where the voice came. A dreaded big bird was sitting on a tree. There were no feathers on the bird. It was a terrifying sight. It cautioned the king that " Look at me, I took that water, but now I am seeking death. I am neither dead nor alive. Nobody knows me. Nobody recognizes me. Nobody loves me. All my progeny has died long, long ago. Everybody hates me, I am seeking death but I cannot die. I am making the people cautious not to drink water. Anytime, I forbid anybody, to take water, I feel a sense of bliss that law of nature should prevail."

"Go back and create the sense of fulfillment and accomplishment and realize that the whole creation is perishable including stars, sun, moon and only the creator is immortal. Remember the creator, the ultimate reality, once you would start remembering God, the other virtues would follow, you would realize fulfillment of your aim of life. That sense of fulfillment would not be available anywhere outside, it would be available in your inner. Remembrance of the Almighty is the passage as well as the destination.

It is not certain that you may continue to rule for long. You can be imprisoned, you can be tortured. Even your own progeny may put you in prision.

People will not recognize you, and they will hate you." The king pondered over the words and returned. According to the saints no matter how powerful a person may be or the amount of wealth he/she may have, it is perishable. Time waits for no one. No comfort can secure us from death. But the enlightened person or saint enjoy bliss in death but kings are afraid of death. Saints invite death, but kings try in vain to avoid it. Saints consider it homecoming but the king is always under its fear. The animals, birds have no fear of death on the other side enlightened person also do not have any fear of death.

Human beings cannot deplete their consciousness to the level of animals, but human beings can develop their consciousness into superconsciousness.

In the words of mystics, this super consciousness and enlightenenedness is available in the inner.

Always remember the Creator,

Creator is permanent,

Creation is perishable.

22

No Desire for Results

There is a story that a faqir was going to meet God. While going towards God he met two persons who were meditating. When the first meditator became aware that this faqir was going to meet God, he said that you must enquire from God that how much time is required for my enlightenedness.

The second meditator continued meditation and did not care for the faqir or about his meeting with God. The faqir himself went to the second meditator and said that may I also enquire how much time is required for your enlightedness but still the meditator did not show any interest in such an enquiry. He only said, "I have no question.

I am not interested in results. I am enjoying meditation. Remembrance is the ultimate reality."

When the faqir returned after meeting God the first saint enquired what was God's answer to his question. The Faqir replied that he will have to meditate for the years equal to the number of leaves on this particular tree. He was upset and immediately left meditation. Then he went to the other saint, and told him that though he had not asked him but he had also enquired the time required for enlightenment for you but God told that he would also have to meditate for the years equal to the leaves of this tree.

Though the meditator was calm but once he listened to this, he started dancing and singing with pleasure, why equal to the years, of this tree only there are a number of trees everywhere I would continue meditating. I am not interested in results. I am enjoying meditating in the name of the Creator. But instantly the second saint was enlightened.

The meditator found change in the transformation with every meditation. The meditator is never interested in results. The bliss is related to the soul. It develops in stages. Laughter is related to the brain, joy is related to the mind laughter and joy is in limits, bliss is not in limits, as bliss is related to the soul. Soul may be enjoying bliss even in pain and physical problems. The saints remained calm even when they were tortured and attained martyrdom. But worldly comforts are related to mind and these comforts are meaningless for the soul. According to mystics there are five senses in the human being but these five senses cannot realize – the super soul. It is the sixth sense that is based on meditation or remembrance of the Creator. This is not available anywhere outside but it is available in the innerself of everybody and is based on the transformation of the innerself.

Religions were not made by God. There are differences in religious practices but all religions believe in one Creator. Jews and Christians were staunch opponents – of what? but they had the same view of their Creator. As creator is only one, the paths may be different but spirituality is also one.

In the second world war Hitler, Mussolini were on one side, Churchill and Trueman were on the other side, but all were seeking help of the same God for their victory. Religious books are the experiences of the saints, and these experiences are the same for every saint.

According to mystics a human being on the spiritual track will not hurt the feelings of other human beings. Hurting the feelings of anyone is hurting the Creator who is in the innerself. The mind cannot have any idea beyond worldly comforts and luxuries, but the soul looks beyond the worldly comforts and concentrates on remembrance of the creator.

Always remember the Creator,

Creator is permanent,

Creation is perishable.

23
Puzzle in Logic

Once many philosophers were discussing the existence of God, whether there is a Creator of this universe or not. Most of them extended arguments to prove that there was a Creator because there cannot be any creation without some force and it is logical also. They felt that the name of that Creator may be different, but Creator is one and that Creator is solely responsible for creation. They were giving a number of examples with their powerful ideas and logic.

But others, though their number was small suggested that there is no Creator. The process of creation is an automatic process of constant evolution. They had their own arguments and logic.

But ultimately it was concluded that there is some force and there is a Creator. The others who were opposing the existence of God yielded to the logic of the majority, and it was the conclusion of the assembly that there is a Creator who is God. They declared this decision from the stage.

But when they were about to disperse after these long deliberations a child who had been listening to this discussion came there and he simply posed a question that if God had made this creation then who had created God. All the learned philosophers kept quiet and looked at each other and dispersed. They had no answers to the child's question.

According to mystics, logic is related to creation. But spirituality is not related to any logic and the Creator is the centre that is why every part of creation is inclined towards its centre or origin. Spirituality starts where logic ends. Logic is related to mind, spirituality is related to the soul.

In the words of mystics, there was something before the beginning, and there will be something after the end. But no logic can explain it. No logic can explain what was there before the beginning and what shall be there after the end. These are the questions of mind these are not the questions of the soul. Beginning and end of the Creator cannot be explained by logic. Human thinking is confined to mind and it is limited.

The Creator is beyond our thinking. According to saints, the Creator originated from self and is not dependent on anybody. Creator has no form but creation is in forms but all these features of spirituality are beyond logic.

In the words of the saints, faith asks no questions. Questions are related to mind, spirituality and faith have no question as it is related to the soul.

Devotional music is enjoyed by human beings. Devotional music without one Creator is meaningless, why music is enjoyed cannot be explained with logic.

The external is related to mind. But spiritual experience is related to the soul that is in the innerself. Worldly wealth can purchase material goods. But material goods cannot purchase spiritual wealth.

Always remember the Creator,

Creator is permanent,

Creation is perishable.

24

No Explanation
of Miracles

In the last quarter of the 20th century, there was news that in the Garhwal area of India a person died in a rather strange way. It was reported that a saint was living there. He used to sell sweets to the children. Most of the time he remained silent but he was playing and talking with children. He was always contented and enjoyed perfect bliss and glow of aura on his face.

One day a strange light erupted from his *dhuni*. It was of strange colour and of strange fragrance. He lay on the carpet in the room. The light continued and people gathered there to see the light. Ultimately his whole body was consumed by the light.

Strangely no remains of the body were left, either of the bones or of flesh. There was no ash. The carpet on which he lay was intact, light seemed to have no effect on it. Nothing was visible and there were no remains of that saint or *baba*.

Such miracles are happening at many times at different places of the world. But the miracles are not related to logic. No logic could explain such miracles. Such miracles may be called supernatural phenomena. The person knowing some natural secrets can never claim that they know anything.

The saints had stated that the person on the spiritual track never asks any question about spirituality. He looks content with his work – the work of meditation, remembering the Creator. There is one door and one path to reach that door and– the spiritual path is the ladder.

Self Realization – enlightenedness is the goal of the inner traveller, who remains confined to cover the inner distance his entire life. The saints believe that the traveller on the inner path is not concerned with results. Divine knowledge is realization. It is the same for everyone. Living beings are living in God and God is living in every living being.

The same Creator is residing in every particle of creation and all particles reside in the Creator. Human beings gather outward material of comfort for their inner peace. But inner peace is not concerned with outward material comforts. In the words of mystics the centre of every soul – is the centre of the super soul.

According to mystics the Creator is in every particle and the Creator is separate also. Every soul originates from the Creator and every soul is separate also. Every soul strives to join the super soul – the Creator.

Always remember the Creator,

Creator is permanent,

Creation is perishable.

25

Gold in the Courtyard

There was a man who had lived on a hill. He was very fond of gold and gold ornaments. He was always restless in its pursuit. He travelled to different parts of the world to earn money and with his profits would buy more gold and gold ornaments.

He would return home and after resting for a few days, he would travel to the other direction on his pursuit to earn more. He went to different hills, plains, cities, and faraway places and countries.

But in all these years and with very hard labour he could not store much gold. Now he had become old but still his temptation to gather more and more gold did not deplete. He continued his efforts in his advanced age also.

When he passed away, his family members and other relatives sought to bury him in his courtyard. When they started digging, they found a lot of gold beneath the earth in his own courtyard. His family members and relatives regretted that whatever he had been searching throughout the world for his entire life at faraway places and countries was so near to him, but he was not aware of it.

The mystics have stated that this is the state of mind. Peace is available in the innerself of every human being, but human beings are forever looking for it outside in worldly pleasures. He gathers the items of comforts and luxuries to enjoy peace and bliss but he does not enter to his innerself, wherein lies real peace and bliss.

In the words of saints, peace is in the centre of one's innerself and in his soul.

A number of kings had been followers of the saints, but saints had never accepted worldly comforts, power or recognition offered by the kings. No power, pelf could attract the saints.

Every saint is interested to spread the message of spirituality that is in the hearts of human beings. Some of the saints reached higher spiritual stages but they could not find time to preach meditation to others, but other saints could find time to preach but continued meditation – remembrance of the Creator.

It has been observed that a number of kings had left the kingdom and had adopted a spiritual path as saint. But there is not a single example when any saint had turned a king or a saint turned king had again accepted royal life.

Mystics had stated that the relationship of a meditator with the Creator is that of a wave and ocean. How a wave can know the ocean, wave merges in the ocean and becomes the ocean. Every religion prescribes not to hurt a human being. It is the principle of spirituality. It is the essence of all religions.

The mystics have stated that spirituality is to realize the Creator, soul can realize the Creator. Meditation is concerned with soul. Mystics say that life can be divided into two parts - physical and spiritual life.

The mystics have stated that physical life may have different manifestations but spiritual life is one for everyone, anywhere, in the past, present and future. Physical life of everyone is different. But the spiritual life of everyone is the same.

Always remember the Creator,

Creator is permanent,

Creation is perishable.

26
Great King of B.C. Era

Some children were playing hockey in the ground when they found a marble stone with written inscriptions. It was a tombstone of a very great king who happened to rule over a vast area in the B.C. era. Looking at the tomb everyone stopped playing and read the inscription.

First of all, the boys were frightened that they had hit a great emperor who was famous in ancient history. But at present nobody was aware that such a great king had ever ruled or had lived in this area. The record of such a king was not available in history. Nobody knew that such a great king had ever lived. This is the fate of all powerful kings after some time. Even great kings pass into oblivion.

According to Shah Hussain a famous Sufi poet, after living a few days, all have to leave at the appointed time. Everybody has to leave whether a king or a servant.But saints leave with bliss. They attain a sense of homecoming, the kings leave in tears.

According to mystics, saints know that the world is a temporary place. Service and meditation are two elements of spirituality. If one is meditating, kindness erupts from him, he would start service, to the society. If one is serving society, he would start meditation – remembrance of the Creator.

In the words of mystics the man meditating will not hurt the feelings of anyone. The essence of spirituality, service and meditation both are based on the love for creation. Kindness is the common feature while serving as well as in meditation.

The Saints in different areas are speaking different languages and they are using different names for the Creator, but meditation – remembering the Creator and service of society is the same for all the saints in all areas because it is the realization that has no words.

Mystics describe, the goal of spirituality is the one and same for everyone, that was the same in the past, same at present and would remain the same in the future.

> *Always Remember the Creator,*
>
> *Creator is permanent,*
>
> *Creation is perishable.*

27
Meeting of King and God

There was a king with a vast empire and a prosperous kingdom. But he was a cruel king, he continued his wars till he reached his forties and added other territories. But a sudden change occurred in his mind. He became aware that his life is short and he would have to leave everything. This thought made him depressed. So many times he had been examined by physicians but physically he was found all right and fit. So many horrible scenes of slaughtering and murders of other people and their cries and requests, haunted him and he had very dreadful dreams that he would wake up in a restless state and become frustrated. In the meantime he was told by his minister that there was a faqir, living outside the city in a small hut. That he had some spiritual powers and often met God and was immortal.

Though the king did what he was told but still agreed to visit that faqir the next day. He went to see the faqir. He saw a strange light on the face of the faqir. The king lay a number of gifts at his feet. But the faqir did not see those gifts. When he opened his eyes he enquired how he could help the king.

The king told the faqir that the idea of death haunted him. But the faqir tried to explain that all physical elements are perishable as our body being a physical element has to perish. But soul is permanent. The soul should develop as super soul and it is possible only with our labour and grace of God and to obtain that grace one has to remember God.

The king inquired if the grace of God can be available to him in exchange of his kingdom, but the faqir denied. The king said that he was told he meets God. The king requested that if the faqir could arrange his meeting with God. The faqir agreed to arrange his meeting with God. But the king had to undergo a training for it for a week and the faqir prescribed the course of training.

> "You have to beg for seven days from this locality"
> The king was furious, "What are you saying I am
> a king of this empire and you want me to beg
> from this locality."

The faqir remained calm but repeated that this was the condition. "You think over it, I will arrange your meeting after seven days only if you beg for seven days in this locality."

The king turned down the suggestion and came back. But again the same thoughts haunted him, so many times he remembered the spiritual aura and strange light on the face of the faqir. But it was so hard to beg for seven days. How he could accept this suggestion. Ruling the country on one side and begging in the same country on the other side, how was it possible. While the king faced a dilemma but all the times the aura on the face of the faqir attracted him and the condition of the faqir of begging prior to his meeting with God, haunted him.

Ultimately he complied on the condition that the faqir would have to arrange his meeting with God on the last day of his begging. Otherwise the faqir will be given very harsh punishment.

Some of the people were of the opinion that how could the faqir arrange a meeting between the king and God. They felt the faqir would receive severe punishment.

The king went out to beg on the first day. It was very hard for him. People were very generous. They were giving him alms, the poor were more generous, they were paying more in proportion to their income. They were paying a lot of respect to the king. Meanwhile, the people were thinking that the faqir should not have entered into such a bargain. They felt what the faqir had promised was impossible.

The first day was very hard for the king. He was ashamed to be seen begging instead of commanding the entire kingdom. The next day when he went out to beg he perceived that people were greeting him with regard and respect. They were giving him donations. The people were simple, there was no tension on their faces. The second day was a little less difficult for the king. A change had occurred in the behaviour of the king. He found that people were living a very hard life but they had no regrets. They poured out their love for the king and good relations in society. The third and fourth days were easier. Now he was deriving pleasure from meeting people, he had lost all hesitation of begging. He started picking up small kids, washing their clothes, filled with mud, loving them. Then there was sixth and last seventh day.

This was the day when the king was to meet God in the evening after begging the entire day. The people were anxious to see the result of the meeting between the king and God. In fact people completed their respective works early to see the meeting of the king and God in the palace. By evening people started gathering in front of the palace.

The king continued begging and meeting people till late in the evening. The crowd before the palace was growing. The sun had already set, the king was still begging. Darkness spread, but still the king was begging until it was pitch dark.

People were anxious to see the results of the meeting between the king and God. The ministers were waiting for the orders of the king to summon the faqir, but the king was still begging and he was enjoying a different type of bliss. Even he was not aware about the passage of time and he was meeting people at night. The king finally returned to the palace and greeted the waiting public with a smiling face. He was enjoying a different bliss. Then, an anxious minister asked the king, if he may ask the faqir to arrange his meeting with God. The people waited with bated breath to listen to his orders.

But the king stood up looking very satisfied. His face was shining. He had a spiritual aura on his face and he calmly said "There is no need of any meeting with God, I have already met God so many times. I do not like to meet any other God."

The next day, he left his palace and kingdom and went on a "sanyas." What the king had gained materially, he had lost his kingdom. But he had gained something higher than that kingdom, that is why he left the kingdom, whatever he had gained that cannot be purchased by kingdoms and that accomplishment was not outside that was in his inner. He became aware within a week only. Physically he was the same man, but within seven days his inner had changed. What was most dear to him earlier had become meaningless for him.

Buddha had reached this state through great efforts. In the opinion of saints surrender is the first step on the path of meditation. Prayer is also a form of surrender. It is the communication between human beings and God. Again it is not a physical exercise. It is a communication of soul with the super soul, grace of God is being sought in prayer.

Remembrance of the Creator is not a physical phenomenon. It is the realization of the soul that is a spiritual phenomenon that realization is in the inner.

Always Remember the Creator,

Creator is permanent,

Creation is perishable.

28

Ambition and Memories

There is a story, that of a clerk in a school. He was very ambitious in life. There was a faqir in that locality. It was said that the faqir was holding certain supernatural powers and his blessing could bring a big change in one's life.

The clerk was feeling that a teacher in the school was drawing a higher salary and he was enjoying more leisure also. He went to the faqir and sought his blessings to be promoted as a teacher. But the faqir warned him that his restlessness would not be over even with his promotion. No power and pelf can satisfy the human being only the remembrance of Creator can make one satisfied. It would be better to work hard to accomplish promotion in life and simultaneously enter in one's innerself. On the perpetual insistence of the clerk, the faqir blessed him and he became a teacher.

In that ladder, he continued to seek the blessings of the faqir and he became vice chancellor of a university, education minister, chief minister of the state and ultimately the head of the country. Now the photographs, of the head of the country were appearing in newspapers and he had his relations with a number of heads of other countries.

But again he was restless. He was thinking that the neighbouring territories must be under his control, so he invaded one of the neighbouring countries. But that country was well prepared with its defence, so that country not only checked the advance of the aggressor country rather overpowered his country and made him a prisoner.

The people watched him as he was arrested and rebuked and cursed him because he was responsible for huge devastation. He was ordered to be hanged the next day. While in jail he remembered the words of the faqir that one can be satisfied only by remembering the Creator. How contended he was when he was a clerk. How people loved him?

But now he was the most hated person. The entire world hated him. He had lost all love, respect and sympathy. At night he pondered over the events of his life. He remembered the words of the priest that he had heard in his school, "Blessed is the man who has his work – remembrance of God, Blessed is the man who has his house, the house of the creator, now he was remembering the priest." How contended he was. How he had been guiding him, and now he has been declared as the most hated man of the world, there is a difference between earth and sky.

People were cursing him now. He was comparing the wealth of the priest with his own wealth. He felt that he was much poorer compared to the priest. The priest earned spiritual wealth. I earned worldly wealth, power and pelf. The wealth of the priest is permanent. My wealth was short-lived. The priest was satisfied with simple clothes, simple food, had absolutely no interest in worldly comforts and how he had been disturbed, even with all the comforts, luxuries, power and pelf of the world.

The words of the priest haunted him, "What then and how long can worldly wealth last. "Earn permanent wealth that is long-lasting." Memories are related to the past. Ambitions are related to the future. Now he had only his memories. He had no future, and no ambition. Ambitions and memories are only with human beings. The other living beings have no memories and no ambitions.

In the words of mystics the quantity of worldly wealth may go on thriving but bliss may go on depleting. There is no relationship between worldly wealth and spiritual wealth. A person has to be enlightened, not the nation, one can earn peace by entering their inner and not look outside. Jesus at the cross prayed to God that God may forgive those people because they did not know, what they were doing. While remembering the Creator it is not related to mind but to the soul.

Mystics, Ashavakram, Buddha, Jesus, Krishna, Gorakh Nath, Kabir, Meera Bai, Nanak, Patanjali, Laotizu, Heracilitius, Pythagores, George, Gurdjeif,

Hasid, Sufi, Tantra, Zen Master, Zarathustra and all others had been preaching the one and the same message to be aware and search the self. To Sheikh Saadi all humanity had formed from one light, so we all are brothers and sisters.

According to mystics, one repents, while living without remembering the name of God.

Remembrance is bliss, remembrance of the permanent reality – the Creator.

Always remember the Creator,

Creator is permanent,

Creation is perishable.

29

Faqir Physician

There was a king who had a large empire. But he was always sick and remained sad. He got himself examined by various doctors, but he had no physical problem. No doctor prescribed him medicines though no disease was diagnosed.

But he continued feeling sick and he was fed up with the doctors and his diagnostic results that he had no trouble. Ultimately, he declared that if any doctor would cure him he would give him half of his empire as its reward, but if he failed to cure him he would put him in jail for life. So many famous doctors of the world tried but all failed as he had no physical problem and ultimately the doctors stopped going to him so that he may not put them in prison.

Soon a faqir appeared in the court and offered to cure the king. The courtiers intimated him about the condition and made him aware about his fate, in case he failed to cure him. But he went ahead and looking at the king declared that the king indeed was suffering from a serious ailment and he would be alright if he wore a shirt of a happy person for one night only.

The people felt that it is not a big condition. They could bring a number of such shirts. The servants of the king went to different people in the nearby houses but nobody declared that he was a man enjoying bliss. Everyone had one or another problem. Nobody looked happy.

The servants went to different places every day and approached different people who they felt were happy, but still they were not successful in finding anyone. Weeks went by, but no happy man could be found. It was strange. The king listened to all stories. Every day he listened to different tales, about the people and finding no one blessed with happiness. He compared his position and felt that he was recovering from his illness. But the search for a happy man continued.

One day when the officials were returning after a full day's exercise without finding any happy person, they saw a man outside the village near the huts. He was laughing, singing. He was jumping and it seemed that he looked like the happiest person in the world. The officials went to him and asked "Are you a happy man?" He nodded and said that really he is happy. They asked him where his house was, he said he lived in a small hut along with his family and sometimes due to different situations even they have to move from place to place.

Then the officials asked him that if he could give his shirt for a night he would be rewarded with a part of this kingdom. But the man could not contain his laughter and replied: "I would have been the happiest person to give my shirt to you without getting anything but I have no shirt."

When the king was told about this, he said that he had no problem any more and ordered that the faqir be given half of his kingdom.

But when the officials went to the faqir he declined to take anything, and said that this happiness and satisfaction of the king was short-lived. Temporary pleasure, goods and wealth cannot give him happiness and bliss.

In the words of mystics, there is a difference between pleasure and bliss. Human beings can enjoy pleasure from amassing goods, but cannot enjoy bliss. It may happen that while the quantity of wealth may be increasing but bliss may be depleting.

Desire creates disturbance, where there is desire, disturbance will be there, when there is no desire – there will be bliss. Pleasure is related to mind, that is why it is temporary, bliss is related to the soul that is why it is permanent. Worldly wealth is related to mind, spirituality is related to the soul. The king's pleasure was not permanent. No true mystic has ever demanded rule, power or wealth, but demanded the grace of God and remembrance of the Almighty. Enlightenedness is not a physical phenomenon. It is in the innerself and it is a spiritual phenomenon.

The king will enjoy bliss only by his enlightenedness and this belongs to the soul. According to mystics soul is related to human beings but it is formless. It cannot be seen with physical eyes. It can be realized only. Prayer is also formless. It is the communication of the soul with the super soul.

The faqir was called, the king had a long conversation with him. He prescribed about bliss with inner travel that is related to his soul – where the person wishes to be alone, not physically alone, but psychologically alone – that is the path for permanent bliss – related to the soul.

The next day the king left everything and was not found, later on it was discovered that he had gone, away for meditation.

Always remember the Creator,

Creator is permanent,

Creation is perishable.

30

Faqir's Love
for the Thiefs

Hassan was a Sufi faqir of Iran. One night, he was sleeping in his hut. It was a severely cold night. A thief came to the hut and found him sleeping under a blanket. He searched the hut, but there was nothing to be stolen. Hassan the faqir, was watching the movements and actions of the thief. As the thief left the hut, an idea arose in the mind of Hassan the faqir that it is a cold night and the thief did not have adequate clothing to secure him. He went out in frustration as he could not find anything worth stealing. He may fall ill in this severe cold.

So Hassan got up from his bed and came out of the hut. He called the thief and offered his blanket and said, "I am sorry that I cannot give you anything else other than this blanket. Please accept it as the night is very cold and you may not fall ill."

Some feelings transpired in the mind of the thief. He bowed his head before the faqir and left stealing altogether and became a follower of the faqir.

In spirituality, one becomes rich by giving, though in ordinary life one becomes rich by getting something. Human beings who possess spiritual wealth can happily donate worldly wealth. Kindness has no words and no language, it can be realized. It is showered and it is never meant to provide only material goods.

Kindness is the basis of spirituality, and spirituality is the basis of all religions and basis of meditation. Kindness is also the basis of service. Kindness and love erupt from the innerself by remembering the Creator. It is related to the soul.

In the words of saints, meditation is the remembrance and love of the Creator. Service is also love of creation of the creator. Service erupts from the inner.

Faqir was enlightened. He knew that power and pelf is not permanent. But the spiritual enlightenedness that he had accomplished was permanent. He had accomplished the level where there was no hatred. There was only love for creation. This level in the inner cannot be transferred. It could be earned but by the grace of God only.

In the process of education, nothing can be given from outside, only the innerself has to be developed with worldly knowledge. Spirituality is related to the innerself similarly in spirituality, the innerself is developed with spiritual knowledge.

According to mystics the spiritually enlightened souls are more concerned with the comforts of others than of their own.

Always remember the Creator,

Creator is permanent,

Creation is perishable.

31
Fruit of Forgiveness

There was a faqir living in a hut. Near his hut there was a grove of mango trees. Once the mangoes were ripe, the children would thorw stones for the mangoes to fall. As they were hurling stones, the stones were scattered on the ground. The faqir was looking at those children with pleasure.

The faqir was much respected in the area. A number of influential people of the area visited him and payed respects while bowing their head.

One day, as the faqir was walking there, a stone struck him on his shoulder. The boys were frightened and ran away. A thought occurred in the mind of the faqir instantly. He thought all the children are innocent. Hitting the tree to get mangoes was their intention to get the fruits. Now as a stone had struck him he should also give something to the children. He went towards, the children but the children ran away. The faqir some how reached them and told them not to be frightened but come to him.

Ultimately the children came to the faqir and bowed their head. The faqir placed his hand on their heads and enquired. "As you were hitting the mango tree you were getting mangoes, now you have hit me, so I should also give something to you. Please tell what I should give you."

All the children spoke in one voice "Baba please forgive us." Though the faqir was willing to give something in kind, the children were happy in forgiveness. The state of mind of the faqir was of an enlightened man, who had shunned annoyance and anger. He was happy to see the children. The children were happy to be forgiven.

This is the state of mind of Buddha, of Sufi, or any enlightened person. The innerself of the faqir had changed. His outward was the same but innerself was different without annoyance and hatred but love for humanity.

According to saints, enlightened persons have love for the Creator, this enlightened is with the soul, that is the result of his/her inner search but by the grace of the Creator.

Always remember the Creator,

The Creator is permanent,

The Creation is perishable.

****